D1728022

MY BODY BELONGS TO ME!

A book about body ownership,
healthy boundaries and communication.

Authors - Larissa H. Rhone & Tina N. Foster

Written by: Larissa H. Rhone & Tina N. Foster

Illustrations by: Ashini Dahanayaka

Journey 2 Free Publishing

P.O. Box 1075

Windsor, CT 06095

ATTENTION: SCHOOLS AND BUSINESSES

Journey 2 Free books are available at quantity discounts with bulk purchases for educational, business, or sales promotional uses. For information, please email journey2free2013@gmail.com or visit our website at www.journey2free.com.

To Jhayden, Josah, Ariah, and Zacai - I love you beyond expression.

Thank you for bringing purpose to my life.

To all children everywhere, thank you for being my inspiration.

Acknowledgments

Tina Foster, I am beyond grateful for your support; you never hesitated when I approached you about this project. You have been a confidant, a sounding board, a prayer partner, and a friend from the day our paths aligned; I am grateful.

Ashini Dahanayakai- Thank you for bringing this vision to life through your beautiful illustrations. Thank you!

A very special thank you to my family for your continued love, feedback, and support. Mr. & Mrs. Ricardo Rhone - you've been very instrumental on this journey. Words cannot adequately express my gratitude. Thank you for your continued guidance. I love you loads, brother. Sandra Rhone, you pushed, you reminded, and your belief in me has been a driving force.

Ms. Candeesia Rhone and Mr. Navardo Morrison - Thank you for the harsh truths and your unwavering faith in my abilities.

To my Cohort: Ms. R. Dyton, Mr. N. Cargle, K. Frith-Gavin, Mr. R. James, Mr. C. Grant, M. Gordon, D. Gowie, S. Ford, A. Sutherland, W. Cunningham, M. Burke, I. Nugent. Thank you for your continued support and encouragement - your input and efforts made this project what it is. Mrs. C. S-Bates and the SFSPS Family, Ms. R. Brown, your feedback was much appreciated. I love you all - Thank you!

To my biggest cheerleaders, supporters, collaborators, and muse Jhayden-Ateir & Josah-Amare, my heart and soul in human form thank you for assisting mommy on these projects. You boys are such unique little humans; you both continue to inspire, teach, and push me beyond comfort. Always and forever, forever and always - Infinity and beyond, and beyond infinity my lifelines.

Book Includes:

- Letter to the parents.

- Reflective questions

- Activities - creating safety rules - setting boundaries - Touch I like/don't.

- Terms = proper anatomical terms - penis, vagina, breast, anus-bottom.

- Resources = Websites and organizations.

- Statistics = mores for adults #'s on victims of abuse.

- Glossary - "Stranger Danger" Safe Touch, Unsafe Touch, Private Parts, Secret.

***Poster size charts of the Body (for students/children) with place stickers on the no-touch zones may be purchased @journey2free.com separately ***

Hey Parents/Guardians!

READ this page first!

This book is about PREVENTING CHILD SEXUAL ABUSE!

It is vitally important to have regular discussions with our children about child sexual abuse prevention. The lack of communication between parents/guardians and children significantly contributes to the prevalence of sexual abuse. Parents, it's equally important to teach your child/ren to use the correct terms for each private part. Our children need to be informed about their bodies, their bodies' safety, and their rights, and this information is best coming from you. Without being taught that they have rights and their bodies have boundaries, a child may be too young to understand that the behavior is wrong. (**Parents**, *if a child discloses sexual abuse*, **PLEASE** *believe the child! Give the child the benefit of the doubt! Do not dismiss a child's claim of sexual abuse!*) Discussions about sex may be uncomfortable to have at any age; however, it is of utmost importance that we not only have the conversation, but we must be patient and supportive as children of any gender, age, or background may become a victim of abuse. Prevention is vital; be prepared to answer questions and remember, this is a teaching/learning moment. Take advantage of the time spent with your child/ren, make it fun and interactive.

Most of all, enjoy reading together!

From my heart to yours - Larissa.

(Resources listed in the back of the book.)

Hi friends, I'm Ariah. Here are some things about protecting your body that you should know.

We all have heads, shoulders, knees and toes, eyes and ears, a <u>Mouth</u>, a nose – and other body parts, some that are <u>Private</u> and usually covered by under clothes.

5 PRIVATE PARTS

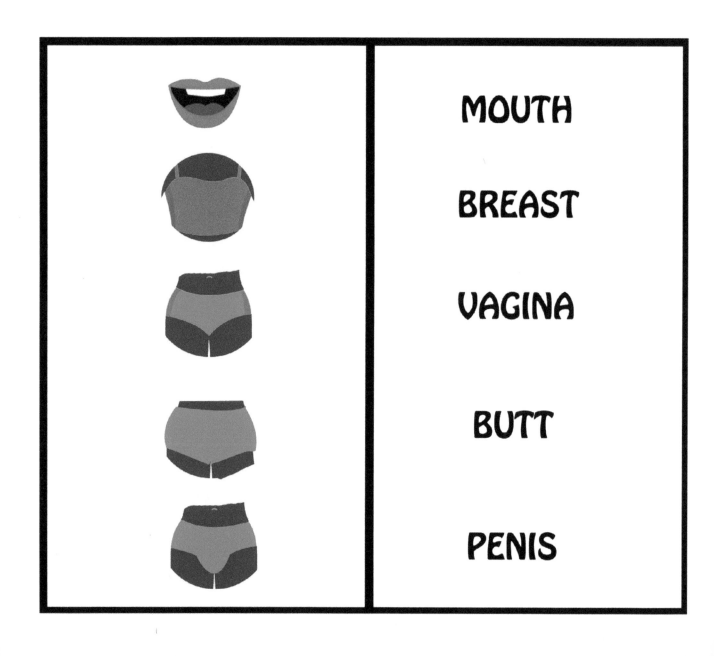

	MOUTH
	BREAST
	VAGINA
	BUTT
	PENIS

People use safe touches to greet each other and to show their love. We sometimes greet each other with a gentle forehead or cheek kiss, a high five, a special handshake, or a hug. Other times we greet each other with a wave, a pat on the back, a fist bump, or a smile...

HUGS AND CHEEK KISSES

WAVES

DABS

HAND SHAKES

FIST BUMP

HIGH FIVES

But, some tricky people might cross the line; if you ever feel uncomfortable or afraid, "Speak up, and tell a trusted adult," it will be worth your while.

MY BODY BELONGS TO ME!

"IT'S YOUR BODY,
AND YOUR BODY
BELONGS TO YOU!"

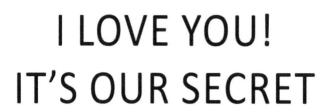

There are certain body parts that should NEVER be touched, even if the person says, "It's our secret" or, "I love you very much!"

Private parts for girls include - the <u>Vagina</u>, <u>Butt</u>, and <u>Breast</u>.

And for boys, the <u>Penis</u>, <u>Butt</u>, and <u>Chest</u>.

THE 5 PRIVATE PARTS

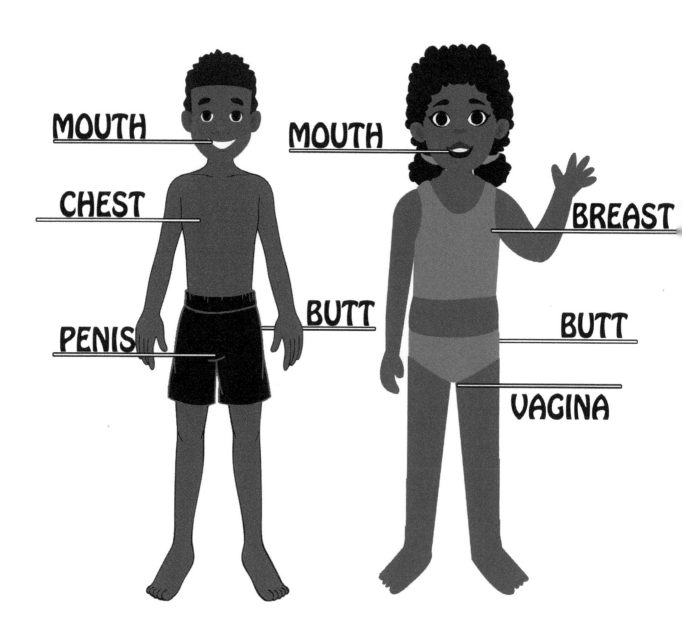

And, do NOT forget, your <u>Mouth</u>,
your <u>Mouth</u> is just as important as the rest!

MOUTH

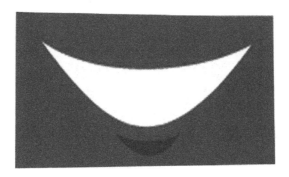

Private parts are special places on your body that are not usually seen. These places are off-limits for touching, except for parents and guardians of babies and young children who need to be bathed or cleaned, or doctors and nurses examining a child that needs to be seen.

Touching is only allowed if your parents are in the room, but if your parents are not and the doctor or nurse touches your private part, it's ok to shout "STOP!"

Always remember:

"IT'S YOUR BODY AND YOUR BODY BELONGS TO YOU!"

If someone touches your private parts and says, "It's our secret," say, "I will NEVER, EVER keep it!" "This secret is bad," and don't *You* worry if they get mad!

Remember: "We are humans, we have a voice, and as humans, we have rights; we <u>always have a choice!</u>"

Children Have Rights Too!

Unsafe touches are touches that make you feel uncomfortable, anxious, and afraid; if ANYONE touches you in an uncomfortable way, You can choose to say, "NO! STOP! that's okay," you have the right to say, "I don't wish to hug, kiss or play!" Because…

MY BODY IS MY BODY!

ARIAH, IT'S TIME FOR DINNER!

Friends, "we've come to the end; Mommy and Jhayden are calling me for dinner."

Oh, wait, one more thing…

AND REMEMBER FRIENDS - 'DO NOT LOOK AT, KISS, OR TOUCH ANYONE ELSE'S PRIVATE PARTS!

P.s. "Do not look at, kiss, or touch someone else's private part either!"

Glossary:

1) "Stranger Danger" - The phrase "stranger danger" was coined to warn children of the threat strangers pose to their safety. However, the term is being phased out as statistics prove that children are more likely to be abused by someone they know that is known by the family. "Tricky People" is the new phrase as this phrase speaks directly to those who appear to be friendly, charming, and sincere and trick children into trusting them.

2) Safe/friendly touch - A safe touch affirms, reassures, is comfortable, and makes a child feel comfortable, cared for, and loved.

3) Unsafe touch - A bad touch makes a child feel uncomfortable, anxious, and afraid.

4) Private parts - These are parts of the body covered by a bathing suit and should not be seen or touched by anyone without permission. The mouth is also a private part.

5) Secret - Something kept unknown or unseen by others.

6) Worthwhile - Being worth the time or effort spent.

TERMS - Practice using the correct 'anatomical' terms.

Vagina

Breast

Penis

Anus- Butt

THE 5 PRIVATE PARTS

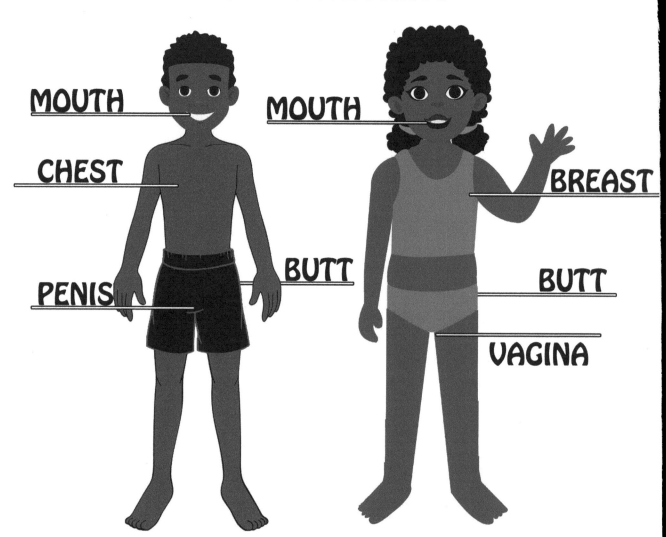

Reflective Questions:

1) Can you name the five private parts?

2) What would you do if someone touched you on your_____?

3) What if someone made you touch his or her private part?

4) Who would you tell?

5) Why is it important to tell?

6) What would you do if the person said it was a secret?

7) Would you tell if it is someone you love and trust, like mom or dad?

8) What would you do if someone put their mouth on your _____?

9) What if someone asks you to put your mouth on their private parts?

10) If something doesn't feel right, what do you do?

11) Can you list four trusted adults?

12) What if it is a trusted adult? What do you do?

Activities:

- Create five safety rules with child/ren.

- Draw/demonstrate.... Safe touch/Unsafe touch.

- Make a chart of safe/trusted adults.

- Show/Tell - What are the private parts? ** see diagram on page 16 or 30.

- Make up a jingle together to help them remember.

- Practice repeating; Children DO NOT keep secrets!

Practice saying each sentence in a loud voice!

I am going to tell!

No!

I do not like that!

Stop!

I do NOT keep secrets!

I have rights!

My Body Is My Body; My Body Belongs To Me!

CHILD SEXUAL ABUSE:

Child sexual abuse is any sexual act between a person and a child, such as forcing, coercing, or persuading a child to engage in, look at, or touch private parts of the body. Touching, taking pictures of, or putting their mouth on a child's private parts, or having the child put their mouth on their private parts is considered child sexual abuse. (Private parts are the Penis, Butt/Anus, Vagina, Mouth, Breast/Chest.

FACTS

- One in four girls and one in six boys will be sexually abused before their 18th birthday.

- A common myth is strangers and pedophiles perpetrate child sexual abuse, but most people who sexually abuse children are family members, partners, friends, and community members.

- About 93% of children who are victims of sexual abuse know their abusers. Strangers sexually abuse less than 10% of people.

- Of children who are abused, 20% are abused before the age of 8

- Those who molest children look and act just like everyone else.

Child sexual abuse is far more prevalent than people realize.

1. **Use the story as a tool** to begin a conversation. Revisit the topic periodically; regular discussions reinforce the message.

2. **Teach children the correct terms for their body parts.** Encourage them to use language that will make them comfortable talking to you. Explain and emphasize that no one should look at, put their mouth on, take pictures of, or touch their private parts - not even someone your child knows and loves. The ONLY two exceptions are health-care reasons or personal hygiene (such as bathing a baby). Your child should not be asked to touch, look at, or kiss someone else's private parts.

3. **Help children understand that they have rights, and their bodies have boundaries**, and no one else has the right to cross those boundaries. **Teach your child to trust their instincts.** If something doesn't feel right, they should get away as soon as possible and tell someone about it. Encourage children to tell a trusted grown-up if a touch, a look, or a comment from anyone makes your child uncomfortable. Emphasize the importance of telling a trusted adult right away, even if that someone is not you.

4. **Establish a "No Secrets" rule with children**. Put a **"no-secret"** rule into practice: If someone, an aunt, uncle, or grandparent, makes a promise to your child and uses the words "it will be our secret," firmly but politely say, "We do not keep secrets in our family." Then remind the child, "We do not keep secrets. We can tell each other everything."

5. **Let children know it is safe to tell. Help each child identify 2-5 "safe adults"** A safe adult can be a teacher, a family friend, a friend's parent, a relative, a coach, or anyone the child trusts or feels comfortable talking

with. Teach children that if they feel uncomfortable or afraid of talking to a parent/guardian, they should speak with a trusted adult from their list. Keep in mind a child predator can be anyone, including someone from their list of safe adults. Encourage your child to tell regardless of who it is that made them uncomfortable or touch them inappropriately.

6. **Practice what to do and say together.**

   Ask: What would you do if someone touched you on your_____? What is someone made you touch his or her_____? Who would you tell? Why is it important to tell? What would you do if the person said it was a secret?

7. **Do NOT force children to express affection. Let children decide for themselves how and what is comfortable.** Children should not be forced to hug or kiss if it makes them feel uncomfortable. Also, If a child complains about being around a particular individual - Start asking questions and *Listen*. Allowing children to set boundaries regarding physical contact will empower them to say no to inappropriate touching.

Be mindful of your actions and your speech around children. Parents, if sexual abuse is disclosed, **PLEASE** believe the child! Many children do not disclose abuse or are reluctant to tell for fear they will not be believed; they fear they will get into trouble and likewise fear their parents/loved ones will get into trouble. If a parent is known to react or speak aggressively, a child is less likely to disclose. Be intentional; do not respond in anger. Children will often confuse anger that is directed at the abuser with anger directed at them.

For Additional Information and Help in the United States

RAINN

1-800-656-HOPE

www.rainn.org

RAINN (Rape, Abuse, and Incest National Network) is the nation's largest anti-sexual assault organization. RAINN created the National Sexual Assault Hotline, which operates in partnership with more than 1,100 local rape crisis centers across the country. RAINN also carries out programs to prevent sexual assault, help victims, and ensure that rapists are brought to justice.

Darkness to Light

1-866-FOR-LIGHT

www.D2L.org

Darkness to Light's mission is to shift responsibility for preventing child sexual abuse from children to adults by providing information on preventing, recognizing, and reacting responsibly to child sexual abuse.

Stop It Now!

1-888-PREVENT

www.stopitnow.org

Stop It Now! offers adults the tools they need to prevent sexual abuse before a child is harmed. They provide support, information, and resources that enable individuals and families to keep children safe and create healthier communities. In collaboration with a network of community-based programs, they reach out to adults concerned about their own or others' sexualized behavior towards children.

National Center for Missing and Exploited Children (NCMEC)

1-800-THE-LOST

www.missingkids.com

NCMEC is a public-private partnership serving as a national clearinghouse for missing children and preventing child victimization. NCMEC works in conjunction with the U.S. Department of Justice's Office of Juvenile Justice and Delinquency Prevention.

For Information, Help, and Reporting in Jamaica W.I.

Office of the Children Registry (OCR)

+1876-926-4079

www.welcome.oca.gov.jm

The Office of the Children's Registry (OCR) provides a professional and confidential system to encourage, receive, record, assess, and refer for timely investigation and curative action, reports of known or suspected instances of child abuse, and other threats to children.

Office of the Children Advocate (OCA)

+1-876-948-1293 or 948-1469

www.oca.gov.jm

The Office of the Children's Advocate is a Commission of Parliament mandated to enforce and protect children's rights and best interests. The OCA office was established in 2006 under the Child Care and Protection Act (2004).

Child Development Agency (CDA)

876-948-6678 - 948-2841

http://www.cda.gov.jm

The Child Development Agency (CDA) is a child protection system with a growing regional reputation for our work in promoting child-friendly policies and ground-breaking programs to strengthen families.

Center of Investigations of Sexual Offense and Child Abuse (C.I.S.O.C.A)

+1876-926-4079

The CISOCA is an arm of the Jamaica Constabulary Force (JCF) mandated to investigate sexually related offenses and child abuse. Formally called the Rape Unit, it was renamed and rebranded to the CISOCA. An office is located in all fourteen parishes in Jamaica.

OBJECTIVES:

1. To create an atmosphere which will encourage victims to report incidents of sexual offenses and child abuse

2. To investigate all sexual offenses that have been reported.

3. To ensure efficient and effective investigation into allegations.

4. To enhance the rehabilitation of victims through counseling and therapy.

To conduct public education programs on Sexual Offences and Child Abuse in schools, training institutions, parent-teachers association, neighborhood watches, electronic and print media, etc.

CPSIA information can be obtained
at www.ICGtesting.com
Printed in the USA
BVHW020921110621
609349BV00009B/2425